NOTES ON FULL TIMING
Equipping & Living in your Motorhome or Caravan

Armand Foster

"Not a motor-home? It's my home and it motors ... Just!"

Notes on Full Timing

First published 2009
Armcher Productions

ISBN 978-1-905672-19-6

Copyright ©Armand Foster 2009

Armand Foster asserts the moral right to be identified as the author of this work.

All rights reserved

No part of this publication may be reproduced in any form or by any means - graphic electronic or mechanical, including photocopying, recording, taping or information storage and retrival systems - without the prior permission in writing of the Publishers.

This book is sold subject to the Condition that it shall not by way of trade or otherwise be lent, re-sold, hired out or otherwise circulated without the publisher's prior consent in any form of binding or cover other than that in which it is published and without a similar condition being imposed on the subsequent Purchaser.

NOTES ON FULL-TIMING

Do you get that Monday morning feeling, or been on the sort of holiday where you completely forget about your home life only to return to depressing reality when you walk back through the front door? We found the cure a good many years ago, its called "Full-timing".
Full-timing is the common name for those people who choose to spend all of their time living in a Caravan or Motor home. As their sole home, it's a life of endless new horizons, a constant feeling that the world is their oyster, a life lived in close proximity to nature and opportunity, an endless pageant of interesting and friendly people.
Living full time requires initial thought and pre-planning, it is not at all like living in a conventional house!
In this booklet we will go through the entire process of getting yourselves mobile be it in a Caravan or Motorhome.
We have divided the book into the following sections;
1. Motorhome or Caravan?
2. Choosing your new home
3. Equipping your base vehicle
4. Kitting out
5. Pastimes, Hobbies and Things To Do
6. Base for contact
7. Keeping in Touch
8. Full-timing Dogs
9. Sites and Places to Stay

Please note before you read any further - if you have a dog who is going to be a full-timer with you, and you intend to go abroad, go immediately to see your vet and request a passport. More will be explained later in Chapter 7, BUT the process takes 6 months so its your first priority!

Something we never thought of till much later but wished we'd done from the beginning was a "Log". I don't mean the DVLC Vehicle type Log book, but a good sized journal book that you can keep a record of each days events, much like a ship's Log. Make a note of everything that occurred on the day, no matter how mundane, it will build up to a valuable record. Believe me you will find plenty of things to write about on your travels but having such a varied life means you will forget many events unless noted down!

1. CARAVAN OR MOTOR-HOME ?

Whether you go down the Caravan or Motor home route comes down to a fairly simple and straightforward argument.

Caravans

The main plus point of a caravan is that it gives you the ability to pitch up in an area, leave your home and go off and explore with your towing vehicle. The trade off is that you have a very long and unwieldy outfit which means you tend to pre-plan your routes and destinations and do not feel ready to explore interesting by-ways and lanes.

We started with a Motor home, then when we sold our house and decided to go full time we changed (upon the advice of others) to a caravan.

We spent a total of a year in the caravan and ended up buying a property in the south of France because we did not enjoy towing the caravan - not the towing in itself but the constant feeling that we were not as free to wander as with the motor home.

You will notice a sign outside virtually every French commune which says "Caravans reglement", meaning you must go to approved sites. Because of problems with itinerants, Caravanners are viewed with suspicion especially twin axles whereas motor-homes are positively welcomed as a source of tourist revenue.

Then there's reversing; you MUST be able to competently reverse your caravan. There will certainly be times when you have to manoeuvre your outfit in tight situations and if you have a problem with this, don't get a caravan, you are getting away from stress, not looking to have a nervous breakdown!

Motor-homes

If you choose the Motor home route you have the freedom of not towing a large and cumbersome trailer. Our 23 foot Motor home handles like a car, it has an excellent turning circle and I have never hesitated to drive down any road or lane that takes my fancy. "What about meeting another large vehicle down a lane?" I hear you cry. Well, in all the years I have been driving the motor home I have only met with cooperation from drivers of other vehicles on narrow roads and a Motor home is MUCH easier to reverse than a Car and Caravan rig! Knowing that you can easily manoeuver your home cuts stress and adds to the 'pleasant life'! The other main plus points of a Motor home apart from being far more manoeuverable are that the setting up times at sites is minimal and when you stop for a rest, you stay within the driving control area so if needs be, you can get to the controls easily as opposed to having to leave the car to rest up in a caravan.

The major drawback with motor-homes is of course that you take your home everywhere with you. This gives rise to 2 problems.

The first is parking and leaving the vehicle with your possessions. Thieves know there are valuables in a Motor home so naturally you become a target. You must choose where you park up very carefully.

Secondly, local mobility which motor homers can solve in a variety of ways:

i) Walking!
ii) Public transport
iii) Bicycles (carried on the back)
iv) Motorbike/scooter (carried on the back)
v) Scooter or motorbikes stored in a built in garage
vi) Towing a small car or motorbike on a trailer or 'A' frame.

This latter option is rapidly becoming very popular. However think hard on this point. We originally relied on walking, public transport, taxis or even hiring a car, our feeling being that if we were going to start towing vehicles, we were back to being restricted so if you want to leave the motor-home on a site and explore with another vehicle, consider saving yourself a fortune and buy a caravan!

Also, remember, bicycles or a scooter are a good idea but do considerably add to your loading, and if you are planning on wandering foreign parts, riding scooters and bikes leaves you very exposed to some incredibly maniacal drivers in several parts of the world!

Basically decide between the Caravan and Motor home but to start, keep it simple. We did and we never found a need to tow or carry another vehicle – although at this point I must admit that we subsequently had to buy a car as our business requires us to drive huge distances, filming sites for our guides. The car is in the scheme of things a "pain in the neck" and for many of our non-business trips, especially European wanderings, we leave the car at friends!

2. CHOOSING YOUR HOME

When choosing your Caravan or Motor-home there are several important considerations: As the overwhelming majority of full timers are Motor homers I will concentrate from hereon in on motor-homes, however, the same parameters will apply to a caravan but with a caravan you must beware of your car's towing capability!

1. Price
2. Loading
3. Design and configuration.

Price.
Get the best vehicle you can afford, look at lots of vehicles, and make your own mind up! Dealers are after a sale and will tell you many things…. but they are not going to live in the Caravan or Motor home, YOU are!

Loading (The Maximum User Payload)
This is probably the single MOST important aspect of your purchase. Loading is what you can carry in the way of goods and chattels AND in the case of a Motor home includes passengers and pets. (Caravan loading is different in that you have to be mindful of nose weight and balance as well as general loading.)
It is extremely easy to overload your motor-home or caravan when living full time. Items gradually get added whilst existing items do not get jettisoned to compensate and over a period of time, it really makes a difference.
It is wise always to be aware of your loading and periodically have a "clear out" to ensure you remain under the legal Technically Permissible Laden Mass (M.T.P.L.M.)
The amount of loading you can use varies considerably from make to make and vehicle to vehicle, from single axle to double axle. To find your <u>Maximum User Payload</u> allowance, deduct the <u>Vehicle Weight In Running Order</u> from the <u>Technically Permissible Laden Mass (M.T.P.L.M.)</u>
It is imperative that you do not go over the M.T.P.L.M figure. It's dangerous, it could seriously affect the handling of the vehicle, it's illegal and has dire implications on your vehicle insurance! The authorities do

check on weights both here and abroad and take a dim view of people overloading their vehicles!

You should be able to find the necessary figures for this calculation in the handbook of the vehicle you are buying – please do NOT rely on the assurances of the dealer that "You can load this vehicle up to the gunnels and still have room to spare." I have come across an instance of a couple who bought a new foreign manufactured motor-home and out of interest put the new vehicle on a weighbridge only to find that the <u>empty</u> vehicle was overweight, i.e., the fixtures and fittings were so heavy that there was no allowance left to carry any personal effects! It happens so be very aware of this!

Typically, the <u>Mass Vehicle Weight In Running Order</u> covers the standard conversion with bodywork plus coolants (oil and water), full tank of fuel, driver (our vehicle allows 75Kg for the driver), tools and spare wheel. It also allows an allocation for liquids, gas, etc.

Your <u>Maximum User Payload</u> is made up of adding together:

The mass of conventional load, (an allowance of 75kg for passengers which is multiplied by the number of seats designated by the manufacturer for use whilst the vehicle is in motion excluding the driver).

The mass of essential habitation equipment, (waste water tank, water heater, fresh water tank, toilet flushing fluids etc.).

The mass of optional equipment.

The mass of personal effects (typical items: food, cutlery, pots & pans, maps, first aid box leveling blocks, tv and radio + ariel, fire extinguisher, books, cameras, toys, bicycles, sports equipment, clothes, footwear).

You can see why it is easy to overload!

Your mission therefore is to get a motor-home with as much loading as you can - a ton is good, more if you can. Remember that the weight of a motor-home is calculated by the manufacturer, i.e. they add up the weights of fittings, fridge, cooker seats etc., but they do not take each new motor-home to a weighbridge to check. YOU must get the dealer to take it with you before you make the purchase or if that is not possible, go from the dealers straight to the nearest public weighbridge and get your new van weighed including the individual axle loadings, not forgetting to get a printout as proof of the weight.

It is also a very good idea to weigh the loaded motor home before you start off on your travels. You may be surprised at the readout and may well have to rethink what is essential to take and what is not. This is VITAL as you do not want to be wandering the highways with a chronically overloaded vehicle.

A good tip is always travel with your water tank near to empty and your chemical toilet cassette and waste water tank fully emptied. This will make a difference to your traveling payload. A litre of water is equivalent to 1kg of weight, and in the case of our 23ft motor-home, having both fresh water and waste water tanks full is equivalent to adding the weight of 2 average size adults to the payload!

Weight distribution is an important factor in ensuring your vehicle is correctly balanced and road holding not compromised.

Load your motor-home carefully with the heavier items well distributed and placed in lower lockers, cupboards or under-bed lockers keeping lightweight items for the overhead lockers.

Design and Configuration

This is another vital stage in your process of getting set up with a home; it must work for you. Everyone has their own specific requirements, likes and dislikes so its worth taking some initial time to decide what is a must (or must not) for you and to keep this to the fore when choosing your van so that you are not persuaded to buy on just looks or best deals alone.

This is how we went about choosing our design of Motor-home. It must have worked for us because after many years in the same van we cannot fault the layout!

We first researched by buying motor-home magazines then contacted manufacturers and dealers to get brochures with layout plans.

Using these we listed a set of parameters that were vital for us.

1. A fixed bed that was also long enough to comfortably accommodate my 6ft 1inch height, not forgetting that when I lay down my feet tend to extend my length to well over 6 foot. (If you are tall, lay on the carpet, get comfortably stretched out and measure the length required.) Remember you are looking at long term, not just a weekend here and a fortnight there, so the acquisition of a comfortable bed is an extremely important factor in whether you will enjoy full timing. If the bed is too short, it will be misery with cramped limbs aching in the night!

A fixed bed also means that you can flop out with minimum effort. Long term, making up beds from seating every night can get really tedious after a couple of months!

Another point to consider [for us oldies!] is having a bed that you can get in and out of without climbing ladders and indulging in gymnastics every time you want to visit the toilet in the night.

2. **A kitchen with as much workspace as possible**, a good cooker and a reasonable sized fridge. We do not have a microwave and happily live without one! However, many people find a microwave useful and depending on the type of cooking you do, it might be a better configuration to have a microwave fitted instead of the oven. There are such models available.

3. **A sitting area that includes the Cab seats.** What's the point in having some 3 feet of cab space and not being able to use it? Both our seats rotate so we can comfortably seat 7 for dinner parties!

4. **As much locker space as possible** including outside lockers. We have a full sized locker above the cab (ideal for laptops and art material), large under-bed locker with outside access for folding chairs, food storage and other bulky essentials and as little shelf space as possible. Again what is the use of twiddly little shelves whose contents have to be stowed securely every time you move?

5. **A vehicle that has enough power.** We have a 2.8 turbo diesel which, when cruising, gets us about 30 to the gallon!

6. **A fibre-glass shell.** I am not a fan of aluminium clad motor-homes. They are lighter but our full fibre-glass body has great integral strength.

7. **Gas**
See Section 9. Sites and Places to Stay/Going Abroad/Gas - page 37. You need to decide which kind of gas you will carry - butane or propane - at the time of purchase so that you have the correct regulator fitted for your requirements. Changing over at a later date can be expensive.

7. **An awning.** We have a simple 3 metre sunshade, wind down side awning. We do not have sides that zip on nor do we need it. We manage within the confines of the camper and remember that as you will most probably follow the sun, you will spend a great deal of time outdoors, so a simple sunshade will suffice.

8. **Other things to look for** are simple things like top locker height. If you are tall, when you open the doors can you see in? Is the ceiling sufficiently high? Too low can get very claustrophobic! Another boon to us is our skylights. We have 2 large ones, one above the sitting area and one above the bed. These are our favorite aspect of the camper – it's wonderful to lie in bed and look at the sky, be it clouds, blue sky or a starry night!

3. EQUIPPING YOUR BASE VEHICLE

Fitting out your base vehicle as a home is a process that takes thought, because you are weight restricted and, lets face it, very short of space. You should therefore aim for the MINIMUM possible for a comfortable lifestyle.
Can I tell you a little story here.....
We met a couple of full timers who had been living the life for several months. They had a large, beautiful, well appointed German caravan, an estate car that was adequate but their possessions were mind boggling. The car and van were loaded to extreme, even to pots of geraniums and a herb garden. We met them a few months later. The caravan had been replaced with a motor-home of similar size to ours, it had a large caravan style awning and their car now towed a fair sized trailer loaded with even more kit and clobber! It turned out that they had had a near catastrophic snake on the motorway, caused by the universal symptoms of an overloaded caravan, excessive speed on the motorway and a passing articulated truck slipstream. So traumatised were they that they had changed to a motor-home! They then went to even more expense of selling the estate car and trailer and buying a small car and trailer (You cannot tow on an A frame in France - hence the trailer.) but she still had her portable garden! Needless to say we got an email some weeks later informing us that they had bought a house! Another couple gave up as she insisted on running her kitchen like a normal home including baking bread daily.....in a hot summer..... They gave up within the year!
The lesson in this is sit down and jointly plan the equipping of your vehicle very carefully.
Starting with the vehicle requirements;
You are supplied with the basic tool kit that comes with the van. To that you want to add a good set of screwdrivers, from fine to large slot to Philips. One of those multi-headed tools is useful but have some standard screwdrivers as well as the changeable head varieties can be difficult when access is restricted. I found a very good multiple tool kit in a DIY store and added to it. Once again restrict it, but with a bit of thought you can carry the minimum of tools to do any repair within reason.
I also carry duct tape, super-glue gel, plastic cable ties of various sizes,

spare fuses, a couple of spare halogen bulbs for interior lights, some bungee rubber straps, a towrope and foot pump.

My most important tool which is in daily use is my Swiss army knife. Get a good one with all the basic tools. Because of the current knife policy in Britain, I no longer carry it in my pocket but it is still in daily use in the camper.

You will also require a length of hose. We have a 50 foot cassette hose on a reel so when possible, we can connect our tank to the water tap to fill plus have a hosepipe with which to clean the camper – along with an extending brush to scrub down the outside and the roof. We also carry 3 buckets, two of which are blue good quality buckets for carrying drinking water ONLY to the van (it is vital that you observe strict hygiene rules when handling your drinking water!) and an orange bucket for general use, emptying grey water, cleaning etc. We use MV service points when they are available but the buckets are less cumbersome than the rolling water tanks and waste tanks you see caravanners using! While on the subject of water, we do carry water purification tablets so that we can periodically sterilise our water tank, plus the ability to sterilise the tank if we suspect that we had some tainted water (it happens when you visit different places!) plus we also carry a spray can of disinfectant for the buckets.

Carry at least 2 good torches/lanterns. Its a good idea to have one of the torches as a rechargeable one and a second torch or lantern that works on a wind up principle. Have a powerful torch placed handily by the door.

Another basic rule to observe is for each occupant of the van to have their own set of keys and to get into the habit of carrying them with you to minimise catastrophic loss or going out, locking the door, only to remember that the keys are sitting on the kitchen unit!

On top of this list you have the mandatory equipment that is required for Europe.

1. Hazard warning triangles.   Get two as Spain requires two.
2. Yellow reflective vests for each occupant.   We have lightweight vests and in Europe wear them all the time as we have met people who have been fined in Spain for putting their jackets on AFTER alighting from the vehicle!
3. A fire extinguisher, in fact we have two, one in the driver's side of the cab and one in the camper near the door and kitchen area. You may prefer one extinguisher and a fire blanket.
4. A spare set of light bulbs for the vehicle.

5. A first aid kit. Apart from being a very practical necessity in its own right, the carrying of a first aid kit is also mandatory in European countries. Keep it in the cab and get a very good one so it covers you for life's little mishaps in the camper!
6. If you wear spectacles you must carry spare pairs in some European countries but it's a good idea wherever you go!
7. If you carry dogs, you should have some form of restraint between the cab and the rear to prevent the dogs getting through or being flung through in an accident. We had a heavy duty cargo net which was fixed on hooks behind the cab seats.
Remember that the vans used as motor-home bases are pan European makes so spares and repairs are rarely a problem, in fact I find the European garages far more helpful and far quicker to put themselves out for you than are their British brethren!
8. Finally, maps and guides. We don't use satellite navigation, finding navigating by map easy and satisfying. This is a personal choice but if you do use satellite navigation, especially towing a caravan, be aware that the sat. nav. does not compensate for the fact that you are towing a large outfit and can steer you down unsuitable lanes. Even with a satellite navigation system, it is still worthwhile purchasing paper maps – but get the best detailed map possible for the countries you drive in.
For guides on areas visit tourist information offices, and check with campsite owners. Don't load yourselves down with guidebooks - they're heavy!
9. Remember with all this you can add or subtract as you go along, so get the basics - other requirements will show up with experience!

"I don't care what your Sat.Nav. says .... Does this look like Milton Keynes?"

4. KITTING OUT THE MOTOR-HOME

Before we start to fill up every nook and cranny with our toys there is a basic requirement to protect the interior.

Your motor-home is a very expensive vehicle. In all likelihood you will one day sell it to either go to another form of living or trade it in for a newer model, so to that end you want to protect the interior!

We got protective covers made for the upholstery, seat covers for the cab seats, and I bought several meters of breathable ground sheet from a Dealer's shop which I cut to size to line the bottom of every locker. On the various overhead lockers I cut the liner to be a good deal longer on the door side so that it hung outside the locker. Once the contents were installed, this flap folded back up to form a cover and protection between contents and door.

We also had the manufacturer of the van, (we bought British and have no regrets!) make us a spare set of carpets which are in store with our few treasured possessions! Yes, one day we will settle down again with a house but not for the foreseeable future - and it will probably be a small log cabin somewhere warm! What you will find living full time is that you constantly see attractive places but then the thought of losing the incredible independence puts you off!

We have noticed that friends and acquaintances both envy our lifestyle but then cannot imagine we are happy without a home of bricks and mortar. We have a home we tell them, it moves, its snug and cosy and when we get the occasional obnoxious neighbour we unplug and move on!

I have divided the equipping of the home into the following categories.
1. Kitchen and catering
2. Bedroom and bed linen
3. Clothes and footwear
4. Laundry facilities
5. Bathroom
6. Living room including pastimes!

KITCHEN AND CATERING
(Extracts taken from "2 Pan Cooking for caravans, motor-homes boats & other small spaces by Cheryl Foster)

Cooking in a camper, caravan or boat should be part of the fun of being mobile and free from the time consuming maintenance tasks that so beset us when owning a stationary property.

With very limited work space, complicated techniques or recipes that require a host of pots and pans are to be avoided, replaced by quick, simple cooking requiring as few pans or utensils as possible – with the added bonus that such tactics minimise the washing up!

Mindful of overloading the weight restriction in our camper we fitted ourselves out with gear that was light and compact as possible, thus I brought a camping set of non stick saucepans that consisted of three saucepans, small, medium and large. Within a mere few weeks, the cheap non-stick coating (usually characterised by a very black, shiny, smooth surface) was scratched and peeling not helped by the light, thin pan bottom which made it virtually impossible to cook on the gas without catching and burning food on the bottom - which in turn required hard work to clean off and added to the ruination of the non-stick surface. I quickly dumped the saucepans in favour of proper heavy duty saucepans with decent non-stick coating (usually characterised by a dull almost gritty surface) but mindful of their weight, contented myself with just two pans – one large and one medium sized. My other cooking equipment consists of a good sized, non stick wok that doubles as frying pan and a non stick roasting/ baking tray. That's it – even if I wanted to go complicated, I couldn't!

Our camper, like most modern British camper vans and caravans, does have a cooker with four gas rings, grill and oven. However, doing a full size Sunday roast, whilst possible, is in my opinion undesirable. It takes too long, uses up too much gas and leaves an awful lot of washing up – none of which is good news in a small space for whilst the cooker may be near full size, the working surfaces and sink certainly are not.

The other cooking equipment we've put on board are two gas rings which on fine days are set up on the camper's table outside. To help keep the wind at bay, we've made a simple 3-sided screen to fit around the 2 burners (some camping stoves have a screen already incorporated in them) and the cooking is done alfresco.

Bearing all this in mind, I quickly adapted my normal recipes to fit the constraints of a camper/caravan environment so that in the main the recipes I employ use only two pans and whilst they can easily be cooked on top of the stove, just as importantly, they can readily transfer to cooking outside.

When cooking outside I try to get all the necessary ingredients for the meal together at the start so as to minimize the number of times I have to re-climb aboard the van to fetch something and whilst invariably there is always something one forgets, a couple of minutes spent collecting all the ingredients on a tray helps cut down on unwanted journeys.

The name of the game is to produce tasty, delicious and nutritious meals with the minimum of preparation and difficulty.

Basic Kitchen Equipment

When I first came to camping, I tried bringing my whole kitchen with me. My husband - used to a lot more basic 'back pack' camping - soon pared down the utensils so that they fitted into the one drawer allocated for the task but even from this I have learnt that in fact I use very few utensils, reducing down to:

Small chopping board – durable plastic for lightness
Small all purpose kitchen knife
Large all purpose kitchen knife - which doubles as bread knife
2 x wooden spoons
1 plastic coated draining spoon
1 plastic coated fish spatula
Potato peeler
Small whisk
Set of measuring spoons
Tin opener
Knife sharpener
Sieve that doubles as a strainer
Plastic measuring jug
Spatula
Pastry brush
Plus the most used item in my kitchen –
A bottle opener!

Besides the utensils and in addition to the cooking equipment mentioned above, I also carry 1 large and 2 medium sized plastic mixing bowls with lids, which double as serving dishes when required. I have also acquired along the way several plastic tubs of the Chinese takeaway variety, which I find very useful for left overs in the fridge or for putting ingredients in for cooking outdoors.

That's my kitchen equipment and despite a love of all things 'kitcheny', I try very hard not to add to the list despite frequent temptation!

Basic Larder

My basic larder is controlled by both the space available and the amount of weight I can squeeze out from the overall restriction on the camper van. Tins and glass are heavy but I try to maintain a store of basics over and above the weekly consumed items such as fresh fruit, meat and vegetables.

In the cupboard:

Bottle of virgin olive oil
Tin chopped tomatoes
Tin kidney beans
Tin baked beans
Tin mushrooms
Tin sliced green beans
Tin sweet corn
Tin of new potatoes
Tin or packet coconut milk/cream
Small packet plain flour
Small packet of castor sugar
Jar of sweetener powder
Packet of sultanas
Tube of tomato puree
Tin of ham
Eggs
Tub of 'parmesan' cheese
Bottle Worcester sauce
Bottle Soy sauce
Bottle Tabasco sauce

Dried spices & herbs:
I have 12 plastic tubs and try and limit the number of spices and herbs - which includes essentials such as Garlic powder, Mixed herbs, Chilli powder, Ginger powder, Curry powder, Garam masala, Paprika, Cayenne pepper, Turmeric, Ground black pepper- to this number.
Salt
Jar of mustard
Onions
Packet of rice
Packet of pasta
Potatoes
Tea
Coffee
UHT packets of milk

As I do have an oven, I also try and keep several packets of part-baked bread rolls in the larder as a standby if I run out of fresh bread. These can have a shelf life of over 2 months.

Fridge-Freezer:

Our camper has 80 litre capacity fridge/freezer with a freezer compartment measuring 36 cm x 14 cm x 18 cm (14"x 5½" x 7"). Nevertheless I can pack away meat for five main meals (the meat, of course, is taken out of its bulky packaging and stored in freezer bags) plus a 450 gms packet of frozen peas, packet of frozen prawns and a small packet of another frozen vegetable within its small confines. Luckily we don't eat ice-cream which would probably spoil this fine feat of engineering!
The fridge itself (always too small at the beginning of the week!) can have besides the weekly replenishment of more fresh meat, salad, yogurt, etc., a tub of margarine, bottle concentrated lemon juice, jam and marmalade, tomato ketchup, mayonnaise and a bottle of (oil free) salad dressing.
My aim is to try to take on board sufficient shopping for at least a week at a time as I don't want to have to keep unplugging the van to go and find suitable shops but it does require you to have at least a rough idea of the menu for the week ahead.

BEDROOM

A great deal of your life is spent sleeping and if you are not getting a good nights sleep, life can be a real misery.
To that end plan your sleeping arrangements very carefully. Here's what we do….
Mattress – Caravan and motor-home manufacturers, for the most part, install mattresses of leisure quality or as one manufacturer rather haughtily told me, 'you are not supposed to live in a camper-van, they are for holidays' so we decided to look at the regular mattress market.
Now the problem is the Camper has a transverse bed space of 7 feet 2 inches by 4 foot 2 inches wide. The first sprung mattress we had made for us from the leisure industry was tight against the camper sides and rather flimsily made, hence we had condensation and mould on the walls and aches and pains from the springs digging into us.
I found upon research that Sealy make a 4 foot wide posturepedic mattress that was 6 foot 6 inches long, therefore a perfect fit in our bed space allowing for an air space on the two walls where condensation was forming. In cold weather, a daily wipe with kitchen towels ended the problem.
We also installed a plastic mesh between the mattress and solid base to give air movement and prevent mould.
Then for the sake of sheer luxury we bought a 3 inch thick memory foam mattress topper to go on top of the mattress! It's pure luxury and surprisingly not at all cramped!!
We make the bed up on the topper, tucking the bedding around the foam rather that struggle in the restricted space to tuck in around the actual mattress.
In making the bed, the bottom sheet is of course a fitted sheet but to help keep the top sheet in place, Cheryl uses another fitted sheet, having first undone the 2 corners at one end, removing the elastic and re-sewing the corners to make a sheet with elasticated bottom corners that tuck neatly and securely at the bottom and a top that lies flat.
We started in the caravan sleeping on the two couches rather than make up the bed every night, which was tedious and I found my hip forever found the gap in the cushions so I constantly woke up with aches and pains! I found the bed short on the couch and very uncomfortable. We also made the mistake of using sleeping bags which are a nightmare when it comes to varying temperatures and very difficult to launder.

(However if you do go down the sleeping bag route, give yourself a treat and use two sleeping bags zipped together. This gives you the room to turn over without the sleeping bag twisting with you and tightening around you in the night like a boa constrictor!).

However, we opted for sheets, a couple of good lightweight blankets and a low tog duvet for life in the camper. It's easy to get the sheets washed in site laundries, and you can use an infinite combination of covers to suit every climatic condition!

CLOTHING AND FOOTWEAR

Once again weight is a consideration, as is available space. We have a small half length wardrobe above the fridge, handy because the fridge gives out a tiny bit of heat and that is enough to rise into the wardrobe above and keep it nice and dry in the winter months.

The wardrobe is shared by Cheryl and I and in it we carry a good pair of slacks, a blazer, a couple of shirts and two ties for "best" occasions for me and 3 smart outfits, a 'general wear' skirt, a jacket and several blouses for Cheryl – and there is still room for a couple more acquisitions along the way!

Most of the time of course we wear casual clothes that are easy to wash and require none to minimal ironing. Thus I wear sports type tee shirts all of the time with a pair of jeans or summer slacks and carry three pairs of shoes, one for best! I even have 2 pairs of cotton shorts – just in case the sun ever shines! Cheryl wears slacks with blouses or jumpers depending on the weather and moans that I only allow her 2 pairs of shoes, although she does have a pair of boots too!

Around our bedroom, we have several lockers, 4 of which are used for clothes such as underwear, handkerchiefs, tee-shirts, jumpers, etc., whilst the large corner spaces are used to store shoes one side and dirty washing the other.

One further cupboard is given over to clean spare bedding and the 3 shelves in the wardrobe provide space for clean towels, winter hats, gloves and scarves.

The point is that you do not need to load yourself up with armfuls of clothes that in the end you don't wear from one week to the next and if you do buy some new clothes, consider disposing of an old outfit rather than continually accumulating.

CLEANING AND LAUNDRY FACILITIES

As mentioned previously, for cleaning the outside of the camper we carry the extending brush, bucket, hose and cloths and for soap I use washing up liquid with hot water!
For incidental cleaning, and to get all kinds of gunge off the camper, carpets, hands, walls, etc., we use baby wipes. They clean everything, even so far as to polish shoes! I really dread to think what they do to babies' bottoms!
I also carry Swarfega Cloths in the Cab for grease. They are also very good for getting black streaks off the camper, cleaning seals that have blackened and tar specks!
We have a very effective little battery charged vacuum cleaner and originally carried a small single tub washing machine, but to be frank found it easier to call into sites periodically where they have full laundry facilities, including tumble driers! For small pieces of hand-washing, we do however carry a wire hook-on clothes horse that hangs on the outside of the camper, also a coiled up line and a packet of pegs plus a small folding ironing board and iron which quite frankly are rarely used! The folded up ironing board does however make a very comfortable rest for a Laptop computer!

BATHROOM

We have a combined bathroom and toilet. Its small but all the necessary facilities are present and it works extremely well.
I would mention a couple of points that make life easier;
Firstly the chemical toilet. We empty it daily so it never gets full. There is nothing worse that getting up in the morning to find the tank full, the weather blowing a typhoon with torrents of rain and you have to go and empty the tank..... with your legs crossed! Then there is the shower. We cannot believe the number of people who insist on using site facilities. We always use our little bathroom, if we couldn't, we would probably have given up full timing years ago! We would say that as full timers, it is essential that you are prepared to use your own bathroom facilities. Not to do so, will seriously impede your wanderings and you will miss out on one of the joys of motor/caravanning.
One tip with the shower is to use it the "French" way, in that you don't switch on the shower on its mounting rail and stand under a deluge,

rather you de-mount the shower head and holding it close to you, soak yourself down, then lather and rinse the same way. This way the water usage and the wetting of the bathroom space is minimal, as is the wear and tear from constant soakings!

LIVING ROOM (Indoors and Outdoors)

Your living space is where you will spend the majority of your time that you are not outdoors!
TV: We choose not to bother and life without television is great - life is for living not living from second hand experience! However we have found that people who have satellite TV which works all over Europe, seem the most contented. This is entirely down to you but believe us when we say that we think giving up TV in the year 2000 was one of the best things we ever did!
Radio: Saying that we do have a radio for keeping up with the news and listening to the odd programme! Make sure you get a good radio with SHORT WAVE reception, and then get the BBC world service channels so that you can listen in when you are travelling round Europe. Our radio is battery and mains so it charges when we are on electric and works on battery when not!
Books and reading: We read a lot, but when it comes to carrying books and magazines, remember they are about the heaviest thing that you will carry, so at the risk of sounding tedious, you have your loading to worry about. So keep a few reference books you might want for interest and the remainder read and leave, or swop! Most sites, even the small CL sites, often have libraries to enable you to do this.
Hobbies: One aspect of full timing is that you need things to do, apart from traveling. Once again the happiest full timers we have encountered have goals and objectives, be it writing, painting, bird watching, photography, and the only aspect of living in a house that is lacking is the lack of necessary chores to do. There's no grass to cut, gardens to maintain, gutters to clean and all the 101 things a static home demands be done. You have the camper to keep clean but its environs is maintained by others so it gives you the time to do those things you always wanted to do but could never find time!
We both have never been as creatively productive as we have been in the years we have lived full time!

Living outside is one of the real bonuses of the full time lifestyle. To that end you want a couple of comfortable reclining lightweight outdoor chairs, a couple of light camp chairs for the occasional visitors, a folding table for drinks etc. (We use the campers folding dining table outside as well as in.)

A windbreak is also handy, although I must admit we got rid of our windbreak for lack of use. This is down entirely to your needs and whether you are going to spend time in the windier climes!

This is also another reason why you want to have a good sized locker accessible from outside so that you can stow and get to the chairs etc., with ease.

Relax in the cool of a summer's evening.

5. PASTIMES HOBBIES AND THINGS TO DO

We now run a thriving business from our motor-home, in fact what started almost by accident has taken over our lives to the point we somewhat mourn our freedom to roam! Quite frankly, if we had set out with the motor-home to just aimlessly wander, I think we would have got bored and given up after a couple of years.

The feeling of freedom is intense, you stop for a couple of days in a site and rapidly feel cooped up, you will find you want to constantly move on.

While Cheryl writes, I do chicken pecking impressions on the keyboard but paint professionally- canvases, not houses! We are always finding things to do, and from an Artists perspective there is nothing more stimulating than life on the move. We also carry cameras and binoculars for wildlife observation.

You should, before setting off, have a clear idea of what you want to do, sitting in the shade, staring into space while sipping Claret has its attractions but you will probably get bored after a year!

Set yourself up before you go. If its art, with paper paints & travelling easel. Photography? Then get a good single lens reflex digital camera. You will be seeing all kinds of things that will be worth photographing and you just might even be able to sell your images if they are good and professional! If you feel like filming your trip, do the same. Get a GOOD broadcast quality video camera, film your trip - people are interested in information on motor-homing. You might even like to talk to us at armcher.com if you make good films that would be of interest to motorhome/caravanners!

Books and reading is great, there's nothing better than sitting outside your motor-home on a warm Mediterranean evening with a good book and a drink! BUT remember the weight restriction, books are incredibly heavy so don't take a complete library with you. As already mentioned, most sites have book exchanges, although I sometimes wonder at what some motor-homers read; still variety is the spice of life!

It's worth carrying a game on board too. We love scrabble - the travel version - it's a great way to pass an evening.

Unless you are on a pension that is adequate or have resources, you might want to make a bob or two on your travels. Remember, everyone who sets off in a motorhome is going to write amazing articles on their exploits and travels and get them published in the Motorhome magazines!

The editors are inundated with stories and other unsolicited matter, so do some lateral thinking. We have seen people doing very nicely making dolls, selling paintings, selling photos, and many full timers take seasonal jobs on campsites, some for a salary, others for a free pitch and hook-up through the busy months. Opportunities and ideas will crop up as you travel.

I have found our travels incredibly educational. We have been staggered at the array of things people are doing round Europe, and especially in Britain. From a man making a fortune selling strawberries direct to caravanners, to a Highland Piper playing in a car park with his Bagpipe case full of money!

You might end your full timing days rapidly having found your Shangri-la up a mountain or beside a Swedish lake, or like us, having sold our publishing business in 1999 and set off on the easy life, now finding ourselves busier than we ever have been - and enjoying it I hasten to add!

"Knitting? .... Knitting! You're going to overload the camper!"

6. BASE FOR CONTACTS

In this day and age, you always need to be contactable and with the internet, disappearing has become well nigh impossible!
For your life on the road you will need a "permanent" address from where you can be contacted, and from where you can register with various, necessary organisations.
The easiest and best solution is Family, where you can register with the local Medical Practice and Dentist, and such organizations as Inland Revenue, Vehicle Registration, National Insurance and importantly your Bank and Credit Card Companies can the send statements, allowing you to use your Credit Cards, (you will know that when using your credit card over the phone or web, your invoice address must correspond to the address the Card Companies hold, even if you request a different delivery address).
A friend who is a policeman told us that without a permanent "home" address we would be detained if there was ever a problem as "Vagrants"! So you will need a Contact Address.

Doctor/Medical/Dentist; To continue to receive National Heath treatment, you must be registered with a GP. If you need to see a Doctor in the UK whilst you are traveling, you may go to the nearest GP Surgery but you need your Medical Card/National Insurance Number to hand plus the name and address of your Doctor to receive an appointment under the National Health.
We have a private dentist plan and this allows us to obtain an emergency appointment with any dentist in the UK that belong to the scheme. This covers you just for an examination and temporary work necessary to stabilize the condition. Normal check ups and permanent dental treatment still has to be done by your "home" registered dentist.
If you intend to go abroad, apply for the European Health Insurance Card (EHIC), the successor to the E111 form. This allows you to access state provided health care in all European Economic Area countries and Switzerland at a reduced cost or sometimes free charge. The card is issued free and you can apply by telephone (0845 606 2030) or online (www.nhs.uk/nhsengland/healthcareabroad).
However, please remember that if you require medical treatment abroad, it will normally entail you paying up front even with the EHIC card, and then re-claiming on the National Health Service. Make sure

you keep all relevant papers to enable you to make the claim!
If you are going further afield then you will need specific medical insurance which you can take out with companies such as BUPA or PPP. Please note that the EHIC card is not an alternative to Travel Insurance and only allows you to access the same state provided healthcare provided to that particular Country's nationals. You should therefore consider taking out Travel Insurance as well (some Insurers now insist that you hold a valid EHIC card) which besides medical cover can also cover you for such things as personal effects, repatriation, etc. Make sure you read the exclusions and decide which is more appropriate to your own requirements/health but ensure you have the necessary paperwork and cover sorted out before heading off into the sunset.

Tax: If you are registered here for tax purposes, the taxman will still require your annual returns and as a full timer, you will most likely remain domiciled in Britain with regard to your tax affairs.
However, if it is your intention to become resident of another EU country, you will need to register there. When we went off originally, we did not intend to return to the UK so we closed our tax affairs here, then when we settled in France, we tried to get our residency, as was our right. "Oh no" said the French, "you've got the right to live here, but we don't want to know about it!" We were unhappy with this so we registered our business in France and forced them to give us our residency so we could be "Legit"! There are stories of Brits who have moved to France, lived, out of the loop as it were, then received a letter from the French Taxman demanding they show some form of tax return from another Country, failing that they get hit with a tax bill based on an income of £30,000! So make sure you get your tax affairs well set up. All European Countries are tightening their tax regulations and for EU residents, Banks, like the Channel Islands including their credit card subsidiaries, are now obliged to give your details to the Tax authorities in the Country where your address is, ie your statement/credit card address. You can opt out of this, but if you do, they will automatically deduct tax from the interest paid to you – as much as 40% and you cannot claim it back!

National Insurance/State Pension; If you are not already a pensioner, to ensure you will have a full state pension in due course, it will be necessary to continue to pay contributions, changing your status (unless

you are continuing self employment) to voluntary contributions. These can be paid each month by direct debit so once set up, you don't have to worry about remembering to pay!
Indeed most of our bills – credit cards, medical & accident insurance and Club membership renewals are all done by Direct Debit.

Vehicle tax: Obviously if your vehicle is registered in the UK, you must renew your tax disc. The renewal notice will be sent out to your nominated permanent address but now the tax can be renewed on line or by telephone by debit or credit card – currently a £2.50 surcharge is applied for using credit cards, so you do not need to find a main post office and stand in a queue! The DVLA will now be able to check that you have a valid insurance policy and if applicable, an MOT Certificate, without the necessity of seeing the physical papers, so all you have to ensure is that the disc once it arrives at your permanent address is sent on to you before the old licence expires.
If this might prove difficult, you may well choose to go to a Post Office and get the disc on the spot but you will need to take all relevant paperwork with you so you will still need to get the renewal notice sent on to you in plenty of time.

Vehicle Insurance: As with tax, vehicle insurance is based on the address where the "vehicle is normally kept" so once again having a "base address" becomes vital!
Places to go for quotes are your Club (The Camping & Caravanning Club or The Caravan Club) if you are a member and also look at the advertisements in the caravanning/motor-home magazines.
Shop around for insurance, and don't forget, if you are planning to travel abroad for long periods at a time, to check how many concurrent days the standard cover allows you for travelling on the Continent. Many insurance policies only cover up to 180 days although there are some that will have no restriction. Also check that you do not require a Green Card if travelling abroad. As a guide, you do not require a specific Green Card in the EU countries but do require one for other European Countries and further afield. For peace of mind, it is always worth a quick telephone call to your Insurer to make sure you are fully covered at all times.
You must carry your Registration Document, current Insurance Certificate and MOT Certificate (if applicable) in your motor-home. The continental police often operate road blocks and demand to see them.

Breakdown Cover; Again, for peace of mind, this is well worth having. Most Insurers will have a scheme you can join when taking out your insurance policy, either their own or tied into one of the big Companies (Green Flag, AA, RAC). Again, most offer some degree of Continental cover, so compare schemes as well as prices.

If you go abroad, it is also worth getting an International Camping Card, which gives a certain amount of protection to Campsite Owners and is often asked for by them before they allow you to stay on their site. The International Camping Card can be obtained from the Caravan Clubs or the Motoring Associations.

"My kitchen tap is dripping."

7. KEEPING IN TOUCH

Keeping in touch in this day and age is extremely simple. We have a mobile phone on which we have a Bluetooth connection to a laptop so we can dial up internet access. We use the mobile for all our phone calls.

The dial up is a back up system. For our main internet connection for our emails and web browsing, we have a Vodafone plug-in 3G card which gives us Broadband speeds (allegedly!) all over the UK. We can also use the system on the continent, however, we only use it for infrequent, rapid short bursts to pick up our emails on the continent because it is still rather expensive.

We have a contract in the UK which gives us virtually unlimited internet access at a similar price to a home domestic connection. We've also had a T Mobile connection card which did the same job as our Vodafone card, but the choice is yours!

For telephone contact we also have an ALPHA Telecom Account whereby we can top up our account over the phone. After registering, you are allocated an account number and a PIN then when making a call, you have a dial up number which when connected asks for your account and pin. This then connects you to the Alpha-telecom network and is very cheap. We use it on our mobile when phoning outside UK, or calling expensive 0870 or 0845 numbers. The real beauty of the Alpha-telecom system is you can use any private phone to call Alpha, the call will be on your account and show up on the Private phone account as a Freecall.

Again if you go abroad, you can obtain the Freefone numbers for the Countries you are visiting so you can phone from abroad on your account.

For snail mail we get our base to forward our post either Poste restante to a local post office, or more often ask the campsite owner if we can get it sent care of the site. We always try to get it sent registered/signed for to be secure - you don't want an envelope containing all kinds of personal post going astray!

8. FULL TIMING CHILDREN

We live full time without children and when we think about full timing, most people imagine a couple whose children have grown up and flown the nest but we have met a surprising number of people who are full timing with their children.
Most educate their children on the move and we have found such children to be well balanced and quite worldly wise due to the travel.
The parents undertake to teach the children "at home" and if you are thinking of going down this road, speak to your Local Education Authority about elective home education. It will certainly turn your children's hum-drum life into a completely magical childhood!
We met one couple who decided to wander Europe for over 3 years with their young teenage children, taking the children not only out of school but also taking the decision against formal lessons for the duration of the trip. When they eventually brought a property in France the 2 children not only had to catch up with the lessons but also learn French as well. Their Mother said that not only did they do this with great gusto, they also both went on to graduate from University and she believed they did much better and achieved more than if they had stayed at school in Britain.

"The friendliness of caravanners is legendary."

9. THE FULLTIMING DOGS

Taking your dogs Full timing is a piece of cake and our 2 large German Shepherds loved the experience. They loved exploring new places, and we noticed had a terrific memory for places that we had visited before On the one hand, they are a very good deterrent for security and also a great talking point when you meet like minded people. I would say that full timing with the dogs was far more fun than full timing now they have both passed on. Will we replace them? Well, watch this space!
Full timing with dogs in the UK poses very few problems. As long as your dog(s) travel well, you only need to ensure you use sites that allow dogs – which is the vast majority of sites, either large or small – and which have suitable dog walking facilities either on site or nearby.
Observe the golden rule that you must ALWAYS keep your dog on a lead outside your van and ALWAYS clean up after them, properly disposing of the "doggy bag" and not chucking it in the hedge!
The other thing to bear in mind is to keep the dog's vaccinations up to date. Also ensure your dog is regularly wormed and especially overseas or in the summer, give them tick treatment. Remember the pitch you are on today with your dogs, tomorrow might have a young family with small children playing on the grass your dogs have just been on.
Vets Surgeries are rarely far away and certainly most Camp site owners can tell you where one is.

TAKING YOUR DOG ABROAD
Basically all you need to take your dog abroad is to get a passport for the dog. This entails a visit to your vet here in the UK, in fact we got our dog passports in France but it's still the same process. The vet will give the dog his rabies vaccine and microchip him, then issues a passport with the date of inoculation. The passport is not valid for six months however because you MUST return after six months to have the dog's blood tested to ascertain there are rabies antibodies in the blood thus indicating that the vaccine has 'taken'. Once this has been done, you are free to wander outside the UK to the Zones or Countries included in the Scheme. When you leave Britain no-one is interested, the ferries and tunnel only mark your vehicle as having Dogs on board. However <u>when you return to the UK,</u> you have to go through the necessary procedure. Firstly before returning, you must visit a vet on the continent. Most people do it within striking distance of the channel ports but

the vital thing to remember is that after your visit to the vet - who will dose the dog with the officially accepted anti worm and anti tick treatment (irrespective of whether you have done this recently yourself), and also fill out the relevant sections on the dog passport - you must then wait a minimum of 24 hours before you can cross the channel. After the first 24 hours have elapsed, you have a window of a further 24 hours to cross - that is within 48 hours of the visit to the vet. The setting of this strict limit on the minimum and maximum time before you cross ensures that the wormer and tick remover have had time to work whilst also ensuring that your dog cannot be re-infected before you cross back into the UK. If you miss the 48 hour window, you will need to go through the procedure again.

When you get to the participating ferry, or tunnel terminals they have an initial area where you are directed before check-in where they check the paperwork is in order before giving the animals clearance to board - with your clearance papers but only when you have your clearance papers, you can then proceed to check in!

Beware of foreign vets! They are all absolutely charming and helpful, but on two occasions we have come unstuck, not seriously, but none the less annoyingly. The first instance was a vet in the South of France. As you might gather from my name, my Mother was Belgian, so I speak French. I asked the vet to do the necessary, also asking him if he was sure he knew the procedure, in fact I asked him 3 times if he knew the drill - Of course he did!

When we got to the Tunnel, they shrugged and said, "no can cross, your papers are not in order." We then had to get a local vet out who, for an eye watering amount of money, signed a form that said the forms we had were the correct forms and in order!

The second time, the procedure had been streamlined and the vet near Bordeaux, again a charming helpful man, was absolutely sure he knew the system. Luckily after seeing him, we were still sitting in the camper across the street looking at the map and planning our route, when out he galloped saying "Quick, give me the papers, I forgot something". It was fortunate that we were still there and he made the effort to catch us or else that vet in Calais would have been another step towards his luxury retirement home!

Crossing the Channel with your dogs is either by ferry or Tunnel. With the dogs, we always used the tunnel for the one reason, we all stayed together. On ferries, you must leave the dogs in the vehicle while you go on deck for the crossing, but the choice is yours depending on your dog's temperament!

One cautionary note on Ticks, which applies to Dogs but also applies to you! Ticks are very prevalent all over Europe, in fact where we owned a house in the south of France they reached epidemic proportions in the warm months. They carry a very nasty disease commonly known as Tick Fever so make sure you dose your dogs with Anti-tick (an insecticide applied to the animals back every 3 to 4 weeks) and keep a lookout especially if you have walked in Scrub, woodland or long grass.

Ticks climb up the stalks of long plants and when they get to the end, they hang on while keeping a couple of legs free waiting for an animal or you to brush past whence they grab and hang on for dear life. They then head for warm soft regions, crutch, armpits or under the dogs belly to start their blood feast! Dogs often get them on their faces after they have been sniffing in the bushes. The main vector for ticks here in Europe is deer, so they are especially common in woodland. However livestock will carry ticks so anywhere livestock roam you will find ticks. we know someone who ended up with tick fever on a Greek island!

For those who have never seen a tick, they are small, flat and brown, almost like a small big bodied spider. They are so flat they are difficult to pick up and once they have buried their mouthparts in you or the dog, removal must be done very carefully so as not to leave bits of tick beneath the skin - make a mess of it and a very nasty infection can ensue. The secret is to tease the tick out, loosen its grip - don't just rip it out! Killing them is best done by putting the tick on your thumbnail and using the other thumb nail to "pop the little varmints!" then clean your nails of the remains! Once a tick has had his fill of blood he will have swollen up to many times his own size, raisin sized if you will, and somewhat blue grey in colour, at which point, he will drop off.

Apart from your dog passport, make sure they have their toys, familiar bed/ blanket, (camper floors get cold, as does Europe. We have been on the Massif Central when the dogs' water bowl placed between the cab seats while we had a few hours kip, totally froze over!). On long drives give them a frequent drink and when stationary, find a good place to put their water bowl where they can get to it and you wont tread in it - it's a small space you're in and floor space is critical. You will also need leads and a securing for the dog when sitting outside. Get the wind-down corkscrew type of fixing, there is nothing worse than walking your dog along and getting attacked by someone else's dog that is either unrestrained or insecurely tied up. Dogs that bother others give dog owners a bad name, as does failing to clean up after them on sites.

The continentals are far more dog friendly than people are in this country. You will see dogs asleep under tables in Cafes and restaurants while their owners eat, and campsites will have dogs, cats, rabbits, you name it outside tents!

Something that always tickles us is the surprise many French people express when they realise that our dogs understand English but look bemused when spoken to in French!

To make sure you are up to date with any/all rules and regulations, speak to your vet or check out PETS HELPLINE - 0870 241 1710.

"Don't look at me like that ... You did it, you carry it!"

9. SITES AND PLACES TO STAY

We are members of both the Caravan Club and Camping and Caravanning Club in the UK. They have a huge network of main sites but because they are expensive, we use them as little as possible, mainly for the opportunity to use their laundries, and of course when their sites are in a location we specifically want to visit.
However, both clubs have a huge range of CL or CS sites which are fantastic, not only are they very reasonable, their range and variety is huge!(See our Armcher Video Guides!).
CL and CS is the abbreviation given to Certificated Location (Caravan Club) or Certificated Sites (Camping and Caravanning Club) These are privately owned sites licensed by the Clubs. They are for a maximum of 5 vans at any one time and must provide the following facilities;
Fresh water point
Dry rubbish disposal point
Chemical toilet emptying and rinsing point.
Many sites also provide electric hook-ups, full toilet facilities, laundry facilities, some even cook you breakfast!
The sites vary from basic fields, to lawned sites to hard standing pitches, and will vary in quality from the basic field with the basic facilities to sites that rival the main club sites. The variety is infinite from urban sites, farms to seaside, riverside to mountain. There are sites that have swimming pools, restaurants, farm shops, marinas, potteries, garages that service motor-homes, art lessons, lakes and rivers to fish, bicycles to hire, the list is endless!
The Caravan Club produces excellent books listing continental sites that are constantly being reviewed and reported on by club members. We have always used them and find them excellent. The books also have excellent sections on continental motoring laws for each country; make sure you study these regulations!

FREECAMPING
This is the art of pitching up for the night in a lay-by or somewhere where you do not pay. You will hear people object to free camping; in fact they make it sound like a crime akin to stealing the crown jewels! We free camp at times and know one couple who spent two months in Scotland and never paid a site fee! They stopped in clearings, lay-bys

then spent 6 weeks exploring Wales and did the same thing.
I cannot see anything wrong with it, nor can thousands of Continentals who do it as a matter of course.
Where free camping becomes anti social is overstaying your welcome - by that I mean staying more than a night. We use it strictly as a night stop/rest break facility. Then there is litter, rubbish and worst of all the antisocial idiots who empty their chemical toilets beside their camper - they even go so far as to park up on beach fronts and empty their chemical toilet tanks in the sea!
So the final analysis is as far as we are concerned, free camping is OK in considerate moderation! One very important point is security. Be VERY careful, you can make yourself very vulnerable. On the continent you are the target of thieves, and in the UK you are vulnerable to "yobs" who will take a pop at campers they find parked up in quiet spots!
On the Continent you are most vulnerable in Motorway Aires. Don't even think about using the Aires to rest up at night - and dogs wont help either if the robbers spray ether through your door vents, the dogs will be knocked out as well as you!
The villages in France have designated Aires where you will be much safer. If we do free camp, we get ourselves into the rural areas and find a spot that is well tucked away. Near towns, if we cant find a pitch, we ask the Gendarmes. They will tell you where you can rest up for the night!
As a contrast, we visited a west country town only to be turned away by a traffic warden who told us the town did not want camper vans cluttering the place up! The canny continentals have long seen Camp-ervans as a great source of tourist revenue so go out of their way to provide for the motor-home fraternity.

GOING ABROAD
In addition to the list of mandatory equipment that is required for Europe (see Section 3. Equipping your base vehicle, page 11) you will also need to have Beam Benders (get 2 sets - its useful to carry a spare set). We also recommend the following:
Polarity tester
Remember the Europeans think we Brits are a strange lot- what is logic to us is a mystery to them and vice versa. Electrical wiring is one such subject where things get a bit 'hairy'.
Polarity varies from site to site, i.e. you have a 3 pin plug. One pin is
Talking to a friend a while back, she was telling me her dream was to

earth then you have negative and positive, or neutral and live, denoted here with a blue neutral and brown live wire. When you plug into a continental site the plus and minus, or negative and positive wires are not always connected on the same sides so you can connect to the supply and find your electrics designed for negative/positive gets the reverse electricity with potentially lethal consequences!
You must carry a polarity tester, a simple plug-in device which tells you the sequence the socket is wired in. You can then act accordingly.
We carry 2 European adapters to hook up. One is the normal one and the other is with the negative and positive wires reversed so that your adapter switches the polarity to the correct polarity for your outfit.
Each adapter is marked accordingly so you can connect and check polarity and check you have the correct adaptor connected before switching the electrics in the outfit on.
Make sure you carry these items and if unsure get a qualified electrician to set it up for you - electricity kills and can cause major fires!

Gas

Butane gas (blue bottle) is ideal for summer but in winter it tends to get a bit sluggish, especially when half empty or less. It is therefore probably adviseable if you are a full timer to change over to propane (orange bottle) unless you are wintering in a warm climate.
We carry 2 x 11 kilo gas bottles. We only use them for cooking and the occasional fuelling of the fridge and a bottle lasts us for about 12 -14 weeks, so two full bottles will last up to 28 weeks - half a year!
The alternative is a camping gaz adapter but camping gaz is very expensive so we used the French bottled gas - fitting a new adapter/regulator. It worked perfectly.
As we often cook outdoors we also have two small gas rings fuelled by cans of 'Eurogas'. Cooking outdoors is to me far nicer than barbeques- I get great meals, not cremated offerings!
Incidentally, the supermarkets in Europe often sell camping gaz, Eurogas and chemical toilet chemicals.

Personal Items

We have found all the major brands sold here, readily available in Europe - the only problem we had was decaffeinated tea (no problem with coffee) and bacon (as we know it). However, if you have a favourite brand, especially with toiletries, it might be as well to take a supply with you. Cheryl for instance uses a particular moisturiser from Boots which of course we cannot buy outside the UK.

sell up, get a camper van, and head off south. She had a dream of parking up on a deserted beach where she could relax in glorious isolation! She is in for a shock; the Continentals are big on motor-homes; they head south in their millions, so you will find beaches littered with Dutch, Germans, Swedes, Belgians, Danes, Finns, all enjoying their splendid isolation! Inland you will however find the tranquility you crave.

Also by choosing your times. Holiday Times and Bank holidays get busy EVERYWHERE, off peak life is quiet, so plan your year. We visit friends on bank holidays or go to CLs that don't have electrics so are shunned by most caravanners or motor-homers. The same applies in Europe; the last two weeks of July and the month of August are pandemonium so avoid the South and Coastal areas unless you have pre-booked!

Other myths are space and cost. People believe that Continental Campsites are ridiculously cheap - we have yet to find them, and as for space, boy do they cram them in, pitches are small and packed in like sardines! Fire regulations as we understand them in the UK do not apply on the continent so you will frequently find yourself in a crowded campsite!

On the subject of "Cramming" you will come across the species of caravanner/motor-homer who wants to park up close to you. It's a mentality we cannot understand; there you are parked on the edge of an empty site, acres of space and lo, some idiot pitches only 2 inches away!

We were in the South of France late October in an EMPTY campsite of some 70 pitches when a motor-homer with a GB sticker tried to get his van INTO our pitch, stopping about 5 inches from our van. I stood outside with my mouth open and his first words were "Hello, do you think I'm a bit close?" He rapidly moved to the far side of the site!

"Perfect .... A nice shady pitch!"

Having said that, I have to say that one aspect of motor homing I must recommend is the people you will meet, from site owners to wardens, caravanners and motor-homers. All, with the odd, very rare exception, are absolutely charming. The range of backgrounds of people you will meet is endless, from Nobility to Professional people to Toastmasters and Chassis builders, a real fascinating cross section of society!

~~~~~~~~~

"Overloaded .... Me?"

Useful Contact Numbers:

H M Revenue & Customs Web site: www.hmrc.gov.uk
H M Revenue & Customs Helpline for Nat. Insurance: 0845 302 1479
Tax Queries: Contact your usual tax office

DVLA (Driver & Vehicle Licensing Agency
Swansea SA99 1AR
Web site: www.dvla.gov.uk
DVLA telephone No. For vehicles: 0870 240 0010
DVLA telephone No. For drivers: 0870 240 0009
DVLA for drivers abroad: +44 (0)1792 786 369
Renewing tax disc: www.direct.gov.uk/taxdisc
            0879 850 4444

EHIC (European Health Insurance Card)
NHS home page: www.nhs.uk
Application for EHIC online: www.nhsengland/healthcareabroad
Telephone No: 08445606 2030
You will need to have to hand :
National Insurance No or NHS No.
Surname/Family name for each person
Date of Birth for each person

Passport Advice line: 0870 521 0410
Web site: www.passport.gov.uk

Pets Passport
Helpline - 0870 241 1710.
Web site: www.defra.gov.uk